you got th

this notebook b

Going for the goals

Goal /1

Goal /2

Goal / 3

top priorities

do it

| ANNUALLY |
| QUARTERY |
| MONTHLY |
| WEEKLY |

NOTES

Going for the goals

Goal /1

Goal /2

Goal / 3

YEAR:

ANNUALLY

QUARTERY

MONTHLY

WEEKLY

top priorities

do it

NOTES

top priorities

do it

NOTES

top priorities

do it

NOTES

top priorities

do it

NOTES

top priorities

_____
_____
_____
_____
_____
_____
_____

do it

_____
_____
_____
_____
_____
_____
_____
_____
_____
_____
_____
_____

NOTES

top priorities

do it

NOTES

top priorities

do it

NOTES

top priorities

do it

NOTES

top priorities

do it

NOTES

top priorities

do it

NOTES

top priorities

do it

NOTES

top priorities

do it

NOTES

top priorities

do it

NOTES

top priorities

do it

NOTES

top priorities

do it

NOTES

top priorities

do it

NOTES

top priorities

do it

NOTES

top priorities

do it

NOTES

top priorities

do it

NOTES

top priorities

do it

NOTES

top priorities

---

do it

NOTES

top priorities

do it

NOTES

top priorities

_____
_____
_____
_____
_____
_____
_____

do it

_____
_____
_____
_____
_____
_____
_____
_____
_____
_____
_____

NOTES

top priorities

do it

NOTES

top priorities

do it

NOTES

top priorities

do it

NOTES

top priorities

do it

NOTES

top priorities

do it

NOTES

top priorities

do it

NOTES

top priorities

do it

NOTES

top priorities

do it

NOTES

top priorities

do it

NOTES

top priorities

_____
_____
_____
_____
_____
_____
_____

do it

_____
_____
_____
_____
_____
_____
_____
_____
_____
_____
_____

NOTES

top priorities

do it

NOTES

top priorities

do it

NOTES

top priorities

do it

NOTES

top priorities

_____

do it

NOTES

top priorities

do it

NOTES

top priorities

---

do it

NOTES

top priorities

do it

NOTES

top priorities

do it

NOTES

top priorities

do it

NOTES

top priorities

do it

NOTES

top priorities

do it

NOTES

top priorities

do it

NOTES

top priorities

do it

NOTES

top priorities

do it

NOTES

top priorities

do it

NOTES

top priorities

do it

NOTES

top priorities

do it

NOTES

top priorities

do it

NOTES

top priorities

do it

NOTES

top priorities

do it

NOTES

top priorities

do it

NOTES

top priorities

do it

NOTES

top priorities

do it

NOTES

top priorities

do it

NOTES

top priorities

do it

NOTES

NOTES

Printed in Great Britain
by Amazon

27789344R00071